To Christine -
In memory of Gammie
Love, Elaine + Yogi
January, 2001

A. Roberta Wiatt

J Wiatt

WRITTEN BY **A. ROBERTA WIATT**
ILLUSTRATED BY **JACKIE WIATT**

V&M GRAPHICS, INC. New York

Cover Design and Book Design: Catherine Lau Hunt

Art Direction: Alessandra Z. Radman

Digital Photo Imaging: Gabriella Kadar

Editor: Barbara Friedman Schechter

First Edition

1 3 5 7 9 10 8 6 4 2

The illustrations are rendered in watercolor.

The text of this book is set in 22-point Cochin Bold by V & M Graphics, Inc.

Printed and bound in the United States of America

Publisher's Cataloging-in-Publication
(Provided by Quality Books, Inc.)

Wiatt, A. Roberta.
When daffodils ran free : a fable of dancing daffodils / written by A. Roberta Wiatt ; illustrated by Jackie Wiatt. -- 1st ed.
p. cm.
LC Number: 00-100580
ISBN: 0-9678695-0-1
SUMMARY: Tells of a time in Mystic Land when daffodils ran free, until they had to take roots to survive the winter.

1. Daffodils--Juvenile fiction. 2. Plants in winter--Juvenile fiction. 3. Freedom of movement --Juvenile fiction. I. Wiatt, Jackie. II. Title.

PZ7.W62484Wh 2000 [E]
QBI00-152

Dedicated to the
planters and lovers
of daffodils everywhere

ONCE UPON A TIME, in Mystic Land, far away, springtime seemed to last forever. Azaleas, dogwoods, and forsythias were always in bloom, and the trees always had fresh, green leaves. AND—the daffodils ran free!! There were thousands of them and they ran over the hills and meadows and danced in the sunshine all day long. They drank the morning dew-drops and feasted on the golden rays of the sun. Their tiny green feet carried them wherever they wanted to go.

There was only one problem with the free-roaming daffodils—if they should fall, they could not get up. They had no hands! Their flowers would dry up and their greens would turn brown and they would blend into the earth, lost forever. BUT—the daffodils never worried about falling for they were certain that it would never happen to them.

THE TREES were the oldest living things in Mystic Land, and there was one very, very old oak tree who could remember when winter visited the land. Very few other trees listened to his tales of wintertime, and of course the daffodils simply did not believe any of his cold, cold stories. They were too busy having fun in the sunshine.

The daffodils spent their nights in the forest where they could lean upon the trunks of the trees and rest until morning. With the rising sun, they once again raced across the hills and meadows and danced in the sunshine all day long.

ONE MORNING there were many clouds in the sky, and the sun was not quite so bright. A strange kind of wind was blowing from the north and there was a very unusual cool feeling in the air. The daffodils were a little puzzled, but they decided to take their morning run and enjoy the day. As they came to the crest of the first hill, a great gust of wind blew across the hilltop and hundreds of daffodils were swept off their feet onto the ground, doomed to die where they fell. Fear and panic spread through the remaining daffodils and they ran immediately to the forest where the wind could not destroy them.

The daffodils decided that there should be a meeting of the elders—one representative from each family—to decide what should be done to prevent any more terrible loss of life. There were many opinions and many arguments until finally one daffodil suggested that they choose a king to help them with their problem. In due time a king was chosen, and his name was Alfred!

KING ALFRED remembered the stories of the old oak tree, so he asked the old tree about the thing called winter. He learned that in the winter it was so cold that flowers could not live unless they had roots or bulbs to keep them alive until springtime came again. When the King returned to tell the elders what he had learned, they were upset. They all knew that since they could run free, they had no roots or bulbs. If they wanted to live through the winter, they would have to give up their freedom and put their little green feet in the earth and form bulbs.

Daffodils had roamed free forever, and the decision to plant themselves in the earth was very difficult. How could they give up the freedom to run and dance on the hills and meadows?

One family, the Spontaneous family, decided they did not believe all this talk about winter. They refused to think about it and continued to run though the cold mornings.

Other families were more worried and stayed in the forest and became very sad. When daffodils cannot dance in the sunshine, their spirits sink and their colors begin to fade.

WHEN THE ELDERS saw the sad daffodils, they went again to King Alfred and begged him to take action. After much thought the King told the elders of his plan.

"There is a great meadow not far from here that has many little holes that were dug by the squirrels and the moles. We must take all the daffodil families and hurry to that meadow before it becomes so cold that we all die. Each daffodil will put its feet into the little holes. Once our feet feel the warm earth, they will be turned into wonderful little bulbs. Then when our flowers dry up and our greens turn brown, our bulbs will stay in the warm earth and we will bloom again when spring returns."

And the elders began to shout, “But how do we know it will work? What if we never bloom again? How can we give up our freedom to run and dance on the hills and meadows?”

King Alfred answered, “We must have faith. The great oak has seen winter and he has told the truth. We must plant ourselves or disappear forever from Mystic Land.”

The elders had to admit that the King was right. They returned to the forest to tell their families about the king’s decision. After the elders had spoken, the families of daffodils knew that there was nothing else they could do.

THE KING decided to lead his daffodils to the planting meadow in the afternoon because it was warmer then. So, for one last time, the daffodils raced across the meadows and over the hills to the field where they would plant their little feet and thereby live through the winter.

All the daffodil families went except the Spontaneous Family, who stayed behind to run and dance until they were all frozen to death by the cold, cold winter weather.

AS WINTER SWEPT across Mystic Land, and snow covered the hills and meadows, the daffodil bulbs remained in the warm earth; and, when spring came again (as spring always will), the bulbs put out green shoots; buds formed; and then the planting meadow came alive with thousands of beautiful daffodils.

NOW if you think the daffodils completely gave up their ability to dance, just go out and watch them on a warm windy day. You can still see them dancing and bobbing in the meadows and on the hills.

Of course, you won't see the Spontaneous Family, but you will see the family of King Alfreds,—and they are still the most royal daffodils of all!!